Anonymous

A view of the contested Points in the Negotiation between

Administration

And the Directors of the East India Company, on the subject etc.

Anonymous

A view of the contested Points in the Negotiation between Administration
And the Directors of the East India Company, on the subject etc.

ISBN/EAN: 9783337059149

Printed in Europe, USA, Canada, Australia, Japan

Cover: Foto ©ninafisch / pixelio.de

More available books at **www.hansebooks.com**

A VIEW

OF THE

CONTESTED POINTS

IN

THE NEGOTIATION

BETWEEN

ADMINISTRATION

AND THE

DIRECTORS

OF THE

EAST INDIA COMPANY,

ON THE SUBJECT OF THE RENEWAL OF

The Company's Charter;

AS THEY STOOD ON THE NINTH OF APRIL, 1793.

LONDON:

PRINTED FOR J. DEBRETT, PICCADILLY;
AND J. SEWELL, CORNHILL.

1793.

[Price One Shilling and Sixpence.]

A

VIEW

CONTESTED POINTS,

&c. &c.

THERE never was a crifis in the ftate and affairs of the Eaft India Company more momentous than the prefent. The queftion they have now depending is, whether they fhall continue to be lords over rich kingdoms, paying large revenues, maintaining numerous armies, yielding the moft valuable articles of commerce; whether they fhall continue to enjoy a regulated monopoly of the immenfe trade carried on between Great Britain and the Eaft, and thus the fineft commercial fleet the world ever faw, alfo continue to be maintained; whether the debts of the Company fhall be put into a happy train of liquidation, and the dividend of the Proprietors

A 2   be,

be, in the mean time, raifed to ten *per cent.*, with the brilliant and rational profpect of an annual addition to their capital befides, and that after paying half a million yearly towards the public expence; whether the interefts of the Company and the nation fhall be thus cemented, and mutually confolidated: In a word, whether the Company fhall continue to hold a fituation far more fplendid in refpect to territorial dominion, commercial grandeur, vaft revenues, and extenfive patronage, than fubjects of any other ftate, ancient or modern, ever enjoyed; and, indeed, fuch as few fovereign ftates could command; or whether, divefted of territory and of exclufive privileges, reduced to raife a trading capital from the ftockholders, expofed to innumerable rivals and difturbances in every feat of their commerce: Incapable, in fhort, as they would thus foon find themfelves of carrying on trade—whether their affairs fhall be brought to a ftand, and the proprietors, inftead of continuing to receive even the former dividend of eight *per cent.*, which was a profit, fhall have to draw forth, by degrees, dividends upon the capital, as the affets

I   of

of the Company, depreciated by its decline, can be realized?

This is, in effect, now the question. Whatever may be said, and said even from most respectable authority, we hesitate not to declare our firm conviction, that, in the possession of an exclusive charter, are involved all those essential interests, and even the existence of the Company as an active body.

It has been suggested, that, without the aid of an exclusive commerce, the territorial revenues would yield a surplus sufficient for the participation proposed between Government and the Company: But what would the Company's share of that participation be, in comparison of the advantages they now derive from the revenue? And since the State lays claim to the territory, and is itself to decide upon the claim, since the establishment of an open trade between India and Great Britain would afford a variety of new channels for the remittance of the tribute accruing to the

latter

latter country, how long may we suppose the
Government would think fit to continue to the
Company a share of that income, in the reception
of which its agency ceases to be thought necef-
sary? Again, it has been alleged, that, with the
great capital, the numerous establishments, and
the long experience which the Company possess,
they must be superior in every market to all the
private traders who can enter into competition
with them: But, besides that their capital would
be extremely reduced, if they received merely an
annuity from the territorial revenue, the question
is not, whether the East India Company would be
superior to their rivals, and might be able, by
the weight of capital, to crush them; but,
whether a trade so carried on would be beneficial
to either party? We venture to affirm, that it
would not; we venture to affirm that, if per-
severed in, it would end in the depression, if not
the extinction, of all present contending interests,
and of the greater part of the home revenue derived by the Government from the East India
trade.

trade. After this, a new order of things might indeed arife. When the field fhould be cleared of all the firft powerful competitors, a more quiet fcene might remain for the humbler adventurers who fhould afterwards enter upon it. Trade would indeed be free, but the markets fpoiled. What changes alfo might have taken place in the country it would not be eafy to fay; but, as the refult of all, we are not afraid of avowing it to be our opinion, that neither would this nation derive fo much profit, nor the ftate fo much commercial revenue, from the India trade as it does at prefent. Be this point, however, decided as it may, it is entirely probable that, before a decifion was formed upon it, the Eaft India Company, left with only their corporate capacity, would ceafe to carry on active commerce; they would then only have to wind up their affairs, to pay off their debts, and, from fubjects moveable and immoveable, to fatisfy the proprietors for their fhares of the capital ftock. To what difficulties, difputes, delays, loffes, they would thence be expofed, it cannot be neceffary to ftate; the cafe of an individual merchant, who feels himfelf obliged to

come

come to a ftand, is a familiar, but by no means an adequate illuftration of what their condition would be. The proprietors will confider what in this cafe the value of their ftock would be, and whether, notwithftanding the actual property of the Company is held to warrant the prefent market price of that ftock, if dividends even of eight *per cent.* ceafed to be paid, and if the capital were only to be realized from the converfion of merchandife and of dead fubjects into money, that ftock could be difpofed of even at par.

This unhappily is not the propofal of a diftant vifionary cafe. The thing is come near to us. A few weeks ago we had a profpect at once the moft fhining and the moft real, of long and increafing profperity ; the hopes of thofe who were the moft fanguine, the wifhes of thofe who were the moft attached to the Company, were exceeded by it. It was a profpect which feemed to give the nation at large content. But now a dark cloud has covered all ; we fee not that we fhall have an exclufive charter at all ; much lefs that we fhall have an increafe of dividend, or a long participation.

of

of revenue, or the continuance of commercial profit, or an affurance of any of thofe things which, united, raifed the Company to fo high a point of view, and their ftock juftly to fuch' preeminent value. What is the caufe of all this? Can we not reftore the flattering profpect which was fet before us? How fhall the differences which have arifen be accommodated? A fair inquiry into thefe points is the fubject of the prefent Tract. It is not, we conceive, enough for the India Company to fay, that the national interefts are fo deeply concerned in the fyftem which their Directors lay down, as that it is the part of Adminiftration to accede to that fyftem.— If this were indeed fo (and certainly, though we cannot fully affent to that propofition, we are of the number of thofe who think that the interefts both of the State and of the Company will be better confulted in their union, than in their difjunction), yet this is not the proper ground for them to reft their caufe upon *, and they go upon argu-

* No doubt there are very cogent arguments of a public nature for an accommodation between Government and the

Com-

arguments extraneous to the conſtituent body as a Company. They argue upon the ſuppoſed neceſſities of the other party, rather than upon the intrinſic right of their pretenſions *.

Neither can we ſo far forget the ſituation of the Eaſt India Company as to regard the negotiation between them and Government, as a negotiation between two independent powers. Both indeed have important intereſts depending, but the Company has its exiſtence. The one has the power of conceſſion; the part of the other, is, by

Company; nor have we any reaſon to fear that Adminiſtration will not ſee and reſpect theſe arguments; but the Directors, in taking this ground, ſeem rather to occupy the place which his Majeſty's miniſters muſt think of right to belong to them.

* Let it not, however, be underſtood, in what is ſaid here, or elſewhere, that we mean to diſparage the ability, the integrity and honour which are to be found in the Court of Directors. We know that it poſſeſſes men eminent for thoſe qualities; and in treating of public ſubjects with the freedom neceſſary for the communication of opinion, we would wiſh to ſtand remote from the imputation of being influenced by perſonal illiberality.

wiſdom,

wifdom, argument, temper, deference, concilia-
tion, to aim at obtaining all that is really effential
to the Company in a new agreement; and if their
juft endeavours to this end finally fail, the nation
will then fee and judge. In the fad reverfe which
has taken place in the afpect of this negotiation,
we fearch in vain for adequate caufes. We neither difcover the real differences which fhould
hinder the progrefs of negotiation, nor trace the
firft occafion of mifunderftanding and alienation.
Whatever thefe may have been, it is not our prefent intention to aggravate them, but rather, by
a review of the negotiation, to appreciate the
points in difpute, and to propofe the means of
accommodation.

In order to form a proper idea of the juftice or
injuftice of the prefent claims made by the Court
of Directors, in contradiftinction to the rights contended for by Adminiftration, in behalf of the far
greater general interefts of the empire, it will be
neceffary to take a fhort retrofpect, and alfo to
compare the offers held out now by Adminiftration, with the expectations of the reafonable part

B 2   of

of the proprietors two years ago. We muft likewife compare the claims advanced by the great
manufacturing interefts of Great Britain and Ireland, with the terms now propofed by Adminiftration for their relief, and view at the fame
time, with a liberal eye, what is due to our fubjects in the Eaft. For feveral years after the commencement of the prefent adminiftration, it feems
to have been annually infifted upon in Parliament
by oppofition, when Mr. Dundas, the minifter
for India, brought forward his budget, that the
Company were involved in debt, which every day
increafed ; thus of courfe haftening on their ruin.

On the other hand, the minifter for India, and
his friends, argued that they were in a conva-
lefcent ftate, and, under the prefent management,
would make a rapid progrefs to profperity. The
price of their ftock, which in peace is the beft
criterion of public opinion, rofe from being fo
low as 118 *per cent.* in 1784, to 190 *per cent.* in
1791, where it feemed to have found its level.

This

This certainty, when compared with the national funds, proved, that the general expectation did not reach 4 *per cent.* as a permanent interest on the money invested in the Company's stock.—— In 1791 Mr. Dundas, after opening the India budget, declared it as his opinion, that our affairs in the East were now in such a progressive state of prosperity as warranted him to say, " That Britain would sooner benefit by a participation of the Indian revenue, than India would benefit by support from the revenue of Britain; and that the day was not in his mind far distant, when the state might thus participate." This struck the House with agreeable surprise, but by many it was supposed to be impossible. The great manufacturing interests of the kingdom have uniformly exclaimed against the Company's monopoly.—— They have complained that their industry has been cramped by the Company's not extending sufficiently the exports, nor allowing others to do so. They have pressed the administration on a variety of points, according to their respective interests; but the great majority of them seemed to

agree

agree in this, " That there fhould be a free export and import trade, between the merchants of this country on the one part, and China and India on the other, in fhips of their own, independent of the Company's control; and that they fhould have leave to fend their own agents to thofe countries, and to employ whom they pleafed."

Some of the great manufacturing towns petitioned Adminiftration to extend our exports to India by all poffible means, and to prevent the exports of India from coming here by all poffible means alfo.

The illiberality and abfurdity marking fome of thefe petitions certainly was great; but there was alfo fo much good fenfe in others of them, and arguments in favour of the ftate fo unanfwerable, that it thus became a very difficult tafk to fupport the Company in their exclufive trade, and at the fame time to do juftice to fo many contending interefts.

Although

Although Adminiſtration ſeemed much attached to the Company, and ſupported them in the defence they made of themſelves, by ſhewing that their exports had been increaſed from 400,000l. in 1784, to 1,000,000l. in 1792, and were increaſing annually, as alſo that the whole of their management was much improved; yet they could not entirely exculpate them. The miniſters ſaw, with much regret, *that this country had not its natural ſhare of the commerce with India, and an irreſiſtible proof of this appeared in the growing clandeſtine trade which was carried on by Engliſh property under foreign flags.*

This trade ſeemed to have commenced about the year 1777, and in 1791 it is ſtated to have abſolutely occupied 10,255 tons of foreign ſhipping (as appears in the Memorial in the printed papers, No. 4.), navigated principally by Engliſhmen, the returns on which from India clearly exceeded the returns of the Company, ſo that the benefit of the larger part of the Indian commerce was loſt to the nation, and this of courſe owing

to

to fome radical defect in the management of the Company. It then became a favourite object with Administration to bring the whole of this commerce to London.

The proprietors of India stock saw so many difficulties started by the mercantile interests of the kingdom to the exclusive trade, as added to the disposition which they conceived Parliament ever had to vest the territory in the state, that all they looked for was a security for their dividend of eight *per cent.*

The minister for India had never given an opinion on this consequential point; but as he had declared in the House of Commons, " That wherever the revenues went, the debt must follow them," the most prevailing idea was, that the revenue would be taken from the Company.

Matters stood in this sort of suspense, when Mr. Dundas, early in January, made a communication to the House of Commons, to the following purport:

" That

" That he conceived the affairs of India were now in fuch a flourifhing ftate, that the nation might participate in the revenue.

" That as the Company had run rifks, and contributed fo much to the profperity of our Indian affairs, he conceived their prefent dividend fhould not only be fecured to them, but alfo an additional intereft allowed to them on their ftock,

" That the prefent revenue fyftem feemed to anfwer very well; and as he preferred the favourable refult of experience to new theories, that he fhould propofe the territory to continue under the management of the Company."

This of courfe altered the face of matters much, and gave the proprietors new and great expectations. A negotiation was commenced between the Adminiftration and the Court of Directors, which appears in the papers numbered 1 to 5, printed by the Court of Directors for the ufe of the proprietors. It began with Mr. Dundas's letter to

C   the

the Chairman, of 14th of January laſt, indicating his readineſs to have the moſt full and candid diſcuſſion with the Court on all points relative to the renewal of their charter.

On the 17th January, the Court ſupplied Mr. Dundas with the paper inſerted in No. 1. ſtyled, "Hints for the Purpoſe of forming an Agreement for the Renewal of the Company's excluſive Trade."

Mr. Dundas's anſwer to theſe hints appears in the printed paper, No. 1. dated the 16th February. He there gives his unreſerved opinion ſo far as he had then made up his mind, but of courſe ſubject to ſuch alterations as might ariſe from the different Memorials and intelligence which were naturally to be looked for in the courſe of ſuch a negotiation.

In the commencement of that ſtatement he provides for this, by ſaying, " As I mean, in the obſervations I am now to offer, to ſubmit my general ideas on the ſubject without concert (it not yet being matured

tured for fuch concert) with the reft of his Majefty's
confidential fervants; *I muſt referve the privilege of re-*
confidering any of the points on which I may have occa-
fion to give an opinion, if upon farther reflection I ſhall
fee caufe to alter it in any refpect." He afterwards enters
at once fo largely into the fubject, and takes fuch
comprehenfive views, embracing fo many different
important interefts, that this letter has been ftyled,
and with apparent propriety, the bafis of the whole
negotiation. All the real and effential points in
which the proprietors had an intereft, appear in
this letter to be conceded to them, and on a fcale
liberal beyond any expectations they had framed.
After providing for the interefts of their debts,
and 500,000l. *per annum* in liquidation of the
principal, Mr. Dundas propofes in their favour as
follows :

Firft, To increafe the capital ftock one million; and to allow a dividend of ten *per cent.*;
which was certainly two *per cent.* more than they
expected, and this upon the whole ftock, old and
new.

Secondly,

Secondly, That government fhould not participate until the above was firft paid, and then only to the extent of 500,000l. *per annum*; after which the furplus to be appropriated in fuch manner as to operate as a guarantee for the capital ftock of the Company.

Thirdly, The government of India, with the conduct and management of the territorial revenues, to reft with the Company, as at prefent.

Fourthly, Mr. Dundas had previoufly given it as his decided opinion, that the trade with China fhould reft as at prefent, with the Company, entirely exclufive.

Fifthly, He alfo agreed to continue to them the trade with India, under an exclufive charter, provided fuch regulations were introduced as would leave the nation no reafon to complain that the exports and imports were cramped.

In fhort, the only terms that Mr. Dundas feems to require in this letter, in return for fuch

liberal

liberal conceſſions, appear in his own words as follows:

". " The ſecond head is a conſideration of great importance, and upon which there is undoubtedly great difference of opinion, but meaning frankly to throw out the opinion I at preſent entertain, I am free to ſay, that, under all circumſtances, the advantages of continuing the trade under an excluſive charter do, in my judgment, greatly outweigh the force of any objections which have reached me on the ſubject of the Indian monopoly; and I am ſanguine enough in my opinion to believe that, when the ſubject is canvaſſed to the bottom, the merchants and manufacturers of Great Britain and Ireland, who are ſuppoſed to be the moſt intereſted in the deciſion of this queſtion, will concur with me in that opinion.— But in delivering this opinion, I deſire to be underſtood as ſpeaking of a *regulated monopoly*, by which expreſſion I mean, that the monopoly muſt be ſo regulated at to enſure to the merchants and manufacturers the certain and ample means of e orting to India, to the full extent of the demand

mand of that country for the manufactures of this; and likewife a certainty, that, in fo far as the produce of India affords raw materials for the manufacturers of Great Britain or Ireland, that produce fhall be brought home, at a rate as reafonable as the circumftances of the two countries will admit of.

" In ftating this obfervation, I am not bringing forward any jealoufy that I perfonally entertain on the fubject; for the knowledge I have derived of your affairs, by the experience I have had in the government of India, has enabled me to witnefs the great exertions and improvements you have made in the conduct of your commerce, with a view to the very objects in queftion : *But the fact is notorious, that a clandeftine trade, to a confiderable extent, is certainly carried on between Europe and India, on a capital provided by Britifh fubjects, both in Britain and India* ; and fo long as that trade continues, the public will not be fatiffied that every thing has been done by the Eaft India Company that can be done, and of courfe will not be fatisfied with the continuance of a monopoly,

I   unlefs

unlefs they are experimentally convinced, by fome
mode or other, that the two objects, both export and
import, to which I have referred, are fecured by
arrangements fufficiently adequate to the purpofe.

" I certainly will not take upon me finally to
form an opinion on the fubject, without a full
conference with you, and the Committee of the
Court of Directors; but my prefent fentiment is,
that the effential objects to which I have referred,
can only be accomplifhed by the Eaft India
Company's *affording an additional tonnage adequate to the exports from Britain and Ireland, and to
the imports from India ;* and this muft be done at
a rate of freight fo reafonable as to fatisfy the
merchants and manufacturers of this country,
that the effect of the monopoly of the Eaft India
Company is not calculated to bring an unnecef-
fary, and of courfe an unjuft, burden on the manufacturing intereft of Great Britain and Ireland.
And I have the lefs difficulty in holding out this
idea, becaufe it is obvious that, if the trade of
the Eaft India Company is conducted on true

com-

commercial principles, they can afford to be the carriers both of European and Indian goods cheaper than any individual merchant or trader can on his own private capital.

" In this view of the queſtion, the propoſition ſeems reaſonable on both ſides: For, if the exporter of Britiſh goods, and the importer of Indian raw materials, can accompliſh both objects at an expence more moderate than he himſelf can afford to do it, he can have no reaſon to complain of the Company's monopoly. And on the other hand, if the Eaſt India Company do not contribute their aid to thoſe eſſential objects, by furniſhing freight at a cheaper rate than any individual can do upon his own bottom; it is a proof that the allegation of the Company's trade not being conducted upon the true principles of commercial œconomy, is better founded than I am at preſent diſpoſed to believe it to be. I am aware that there may be difficulties in the execution of this propoſition, even admitting the principle to be a juſt one: But theſe are more properly

perly the subject of future conference. I am satisfied the difficulties are not infurmountable, and I am fure it is the duty, and it muft be the inclination, of the Eaft India Company to fmooth, to the utmoft of their power, every difficulty that may occur in this effential part of any future arrangement."

The purport of Mr. Dundas's letter no fooner went abroad, than the ftock rofe from 179 to 195; for all thinking men concluded the whole bufinefs was finifhed, *as every reafonable expectation of the Company had been anticipated.*

In the Court's anfwer, however, of the 21ft of February, it will appear that, although they acknowledge the very candid and liberal manner in which Mr. Dundas has given his opinion, they yet are only ready to *receive* all that he propofes for their benefit, without fhewing an inclination to concede on their part what he conceives to be abfolutely neceffary for the purpofe of transferring the clandeftine trade, from foreign fhips and

foreign

foreign ports, to the Company's ſhips and the port of London.

They, in the firſt place, refer to their reports, as laid before the Houſe of Commons in this ſeſſion, on the export trade, to prove that the advantages ariſing from continuing the ſtrict monopoly muſt be greater than a well-regulated monopoly. On a reference to theſe reports, it will be found that they ſay " they have exported a ſufficient quantity of goods to ſupply India ;" *on the contrary, we aſſert that they never had ſupplied one ſeventh part of the goods exported to India,* and we refer for the illuſtration of this aſſertion to a document annexed, wherein the exports of the different nations of Europe are accurately ſtated, and with which we have been favoured from unqueſtionable authority. " That the conſumption of European goods, owing to the religion and habits of the natives, could not be materially increaſed ;" *on the contrary, it is notorious to all the world, that it has been, and continues, in a rapid progreſſive ſtate of increaſe.* " That the conſump-

tion

tion of woollens, an article which the Company had ever amply fupplied, and which had engroffed their unremitted attention, had fallen off much in India of late years, and was ftill declining." *On the contrary, it appears that the confumption of this article had certainly been in a progreffive ftate*; and although the Company, from being for many years in the habit of neither fending the quanti- ties indented for, nor the qualities defcribed, had forced great part of the trade into other hands, *they ftill had fold more in the laft ten years, ending in 1790, than in the ten years ending in 1780; as ap- pears by the Company's records.*

Thefe reports are ably drawn up, if meant to filence thofe unacquainted with the fubjeÊ; but otherwife, to the informed, there appears fo very limited a knowledge of the export trade to India, particularly of that carried on by foreigners, clan- deftine traders, captains of the Company's fhips, and fo limited a knowledge alfo of the demand in India for European goods, as is really unaccount- able. They moreover feem to have taken much

D 2

pains

pains to prove that they had always loft largely by
the export trade.

In fhort, from this latter affertion, and many
others equally unfounded, no papers could have
been produced fo well calculated as thefe reports
are, to prove the bad confequences refulting to
the ftate from their exclufive monopoly of the
Indian trade, *unlefs properly regulated*, on the principles early fuggefted in Mr. Dundas's letter of
the 16th February laft. The Committee of Correfpondence feem to fhew in their anfwer, that
they have no intention to make conceffions, as
appears from their own language in page 14,
No. 1. of the printed papers, *viz.*

" The ideas fuggefted by Mr. Dundas will require a more correct definition and explanation
on almoft every point: In their prefent form
they go to the full extent of depriving the Company of their exclufive trade ; whilft the Company are expected to provide freight for the merchants and manufacturers at a rate cheaper than
they can procure it elfewhere.

" It

" It is sufficient merely to state these facts, in order to satisfy Mr. Dundas that the Court of Directors *never can recommend, and that the Proprietors never can accede to, either of these propositions*, in the general manner in which they are stated in Mr. Dundas's letter."

They are of course, in their first answer, almost completely at variance with Administration upon the points which the latter require.

They propose to supply eight ships, for the merchants to send out exports, at 10l. per ton, but with the exception of naval and military stores.

It will appear afterwards that they did not stop here, but changed their ground, and objected likewise to copper, then to all metals, to pitch, tar, masts, &c. &c.

An appearance of accommodation seems to have been aimed at in an advertisement in the newspapers relative to these eight ships. Freight

was

was offered at 10l. per ton, after excepting against the only articles that could be suppofed worth fending, and at a period well known to be too late to provide goods.

Now can there be a man, pretending to the leaft knowledge of exports, who does not know that thefe articles *excepted againft* were in reality the only material articles of export, and that no cargo could be made up without them? Such an offer made to the merchants, what fhall we fay of it? That it arifes from ignorance; or is it infult added to injury? We will affirm neither; our wifh is to heal. But independently of fuch confiderations, if the merchants had been allowed to export what articles they chofe, no trade could be carried on in exports to India, unlefs as an aid to the imports from thence; for the connection between the two is this:

On goods from India to Europe, the merchant of India, let it be fuppofed, gains twenty-five *per cent.* So if he lofes ten *per cent.* in remitting

his

his money back in European exports to India, which, after paying commiffion, intereft, and infurance, amounting to about fourteen *per cent.* is no uncommon cafe, he ftill gains by the general adventure, fifteen *per cent.* The profits on imports, therefore, form the grand inducement for exports to India, and of courfe as the imports from thence are allowed to increafe, the trade in exports from Europe will increafe in a certain relative proportion; and without this we can have no reafon to expect a rapid increafe of it. The Committee, in their anfwer, are fo tenacious of their monopoly, that they refufe even the liberty to our manufacturers of importing. raw materials; but as an accommodation, they propofe granting bills from India, on Europe, at 2s. the ct. rupee.

The fact is, that bills to a great amount are now annually wanted *on* India, and not *from* it. Befides this, owing to the difcount on the Company's bonds abroad, of from eleven to fifteen *per cent.*; a purchafer of them has had it in his power for fome years paft, by exchanging them for

long

long bills at the eftablifhed rate of 1s. 11d. *per* ct. rupee, to realife here 2s. 1d. to 2s. 2d.; of courfe, even if bills were wanted, the exchange of 2s. would be no inducement.

It is clear then that this could be no accommodation to the merchants or manufacturers, nor in the fmalleft degree tend to draw the trade, now illicit, to the port of London.

The rate of freight, or 10l. per ton on exports, which they fay is lower than the rate of Oftend, certainly is higher than the freight there or any where elfe in Europe. The freight eftablifhed by the Dutch, on their regular fhips, is 6l. per ton.

They take it for granted, in this report, " That the feparate fund or cafh of the Company, about 474,094l. which belongs folely to them, will remain as their property, and form no part of the prefent arrangement." This by no means appears unreafonable, provided they were at all reafonable

2   themfelves,

themfelves; but their attention feems fixed entirely on all they term their own rights, without a regard to the rights of others.· When they anfwer relatively to the claim of Government to the territory, they fay " The Court are neither furprifed nor alarmed at the fuggeftion relative to the claim of the public to the territorial revenues, notwithftanding the very refpectable authority of Mr. Dundas ; as they are, and always have been, ready to difcufs the Company's *fuperior* and *undoubted* right to thofe territories, which have been acquired by the exertions, and at the expence, of the Company, authorifed for that purpofe in a correct and diftinct manner, under the moft folemn charters, and fince maintained through fucceffive wars, at the hazard of the whole of their capital : But as the propofed arrangement, fanctioned by the opinion of all parties, and of the public, will leave the territory in the hands of the Company, fubject, as at prefent, to the control of the board of commiffioners, their rights and privileges will be referved to them entire, and thereby any farther difcuffion on this

E   fubject

subject becomes unneceſſary. In reſpect to the Commutation Act, the Court entertained a doubt whether Mr. Dundas has viewed this ſubject in ſo comprehenſive a manner as he is accuſtomed to view all others." Without entering into the merits or demerits of the claim, it muſt be owned that in this and in other parts of their anſwers, there is a controverſial, tenacious air, which is not calculated to recommend even truth, nor the moſt ſuitable to the character of petitioners.

On the 25th February Mr. Dundas brought his budget before the Houſe, in which was a ſtatement of the Company's affairs, as drawn out by the Court. The eſtimated annual ſurplus of the revenue they rated at   - -   £ 1,621,050

And the amount received in India for ſale of imports, and certificates for officers privilege, at   - - -   350,000

Surplus at the diſpoſal of the Governor-general in council   £ 1,971,050

In theſe they certainly did not mean to over-value any thing. Their ſentiments of revenue would

would be too extenfive a field to enter upon;
but as in the fale of exports there can be no intri-
cacy, we fhall juft touch on the lofs they make to
arife on them. The coft of goods and ftores has
lately exceeded to India *per annum*   £ 400,000

And the amount received for certificates, as by appendix to the budget,
G, on an average of five years, ending   46,140
in 1790-1, was   -   -

And as, from the preceding ftatement, they
only value the fale of thefe exports and cafh received for certificates together, at 350,000l. they
thus appear to have loft 100,000l. *per annum* on
their exports of 400,000l.: If this was really fo,
how can we account for their wifhing to continue
fuch a lofing monopoly? One fact we certainly
have before us—that from the commencement of
their reports, No. 1, 2, and 3, on the export
trade, to the end of them, they infift that they
have loft largely every year by the exports,
and furnifh a variety of ftatements to prove it.
This is corroborated by the prefent ftatement

E 2   given

given in by Mr. Dundas in his budget, in which they make their lofs 100,000l. on 400,000l. Now if it be true that the Company lofe 25 *per cent.* upon their exports, whether charging them with commiffion and intereft or not, and if private traders lofe, not even, with thofe expences and infurance accumulated, more than ten *per cent.* if fo much; if private adventurers, in fhort, do not lofe twenty-five *per cent.* which we pronounce to be impoffible, becaufe with fuch a lofs the clandeftine trade muft long fince have ceafed; then we may certainly conclude that there has been mifmanagement in this branch, and that the exclufive trade, in as far as it has been carried on in exports, has been feverely prejudicial to the intereft of the Company.

Mr. Dundas knowing that, if he erred in taking their ftatement of furplus, it would be erring on the fafe fide, made his appropriation of the amount only according to their ftatement, and after providing for the intereft of their debts, for ten *per cent.* dividend on their capital (as intended to be
increafed

increafed to fix millions), and 500,000l. *per ann.* for the liquidation of the principal of their debt; he then propofes the refidue to be given to Government, to the extent of 500,000l. if fo much remain, and if more, the furplus to be lodged with Government, as a finking fund for the fecurity of the proprietors. The operation of his appropriation appears in letter N of the budget.

On the fixth of March it appears, in the printed paper, No. 2. that the Court petitioned Parliament for a renewal of their exclufive charter, and on the twelfth, that a Committee of Correfpondence had had a conference with Mr. Pitt and Mr. Dundas, of which the committee make a report on the 18th to the Court. The great points which the committee mark to have formed the fubftance of this conference appear exactly confonant to the tenor of the firft letter of the 16th February, from Mr. Dundas, and are thus noticed by the committee, in page 9, No. 2. " They (the Minifters) appear to be impreffed with a defire of

5   extend-

extending the exports and imports *to* and *from* India, including thofe of private trade, by all poffible means.

" That the exports from Europe fhould be combined in a certain degree, more or lefs, with the import of goods from India.

" That meafures fhould be adopted to convert the clandeftine trade into a fair, regular traffic, through the medium of the Company.

" And that the charge of feven *per cent.* which the proprietors of private trade pay to the Company at prefent, fhould be moderated."

The next letter we fhall touch on, as being fingular, is from the Chairman to Mr. Dundas, dated the 21ft March, being the firft letter in No. 3. He is directed, he fays, to fuggeft, that they " neither think it reafonable nor juft to reduce the charge on private trade below five *per cent.*"

In

In the Court's report of the 21ſt July 1791, in which they deeply inveſtigate this ſubjeĉt, they make the charges to coſt them two *per cent*. Now Mr. Dundas propoſed to allow them three *per cent*.; but "they think it would be neither reaſonable nor juſt to take leſs than five *per cent*." for what coſts them two *per cent*.

The Chairman goes on to ſay, "that the Company had propoſed to accept of 22l. freight out and home, to facilitate every reaſonable expeĉt- ation, not only becauſe it wàs leſs than it coſt the Company, but alſo becauſe individuals paid more at Oſtend; but if a further ſacrifice was neceſſary, the committee would recommend to take 20l. in peace, but not in the proportion of 5l. out and 15l. home; for, in ſuch caſe, individuals, after paying 5l. out on the Company's ſhips, would bring their returns from India in foreign ſhips, if a cheaper freight ſhould offer, thereby furniſh- ing ſubſtantial means for extending the clandeſ- tine trade, which all parties were deſirous to ſup- preſs."

Now

Now in a former part, already mentioned, they fay that 10l. per ton out is lefs than is paid at Oftend on exports (of the value probably of 50l. or 60l.); then from whence draw they a conclufion, that thefe fhips would bring goods home, valuing from 500l. to 600l. per ton, at a lefs freight than 15l. ? Befides, did they not know that there was a difference of one *per cent.* in the infurance, equal of courfe to 5l. or 6l. per ton, after allowing for which, they muft know that 10l. on a foreign fhip coft a merchant equal to 15l. upon a Company's fhip ?

When we weigh this with the thorough invef-tigation made in the Court's report of 21ft of July 1791, and in a former report equally well drawn up on freight of privileged goods, where they determine " that the freight paid by the Company on all their piece goods amounted to 51l. per ton, it is not eafy to fuggeft why they fhould apprehend that foreign fhips would bring fimilar goods under 15l. per ton.

On the 22d, Mr. Dundas enclofed to the Chairman fuggeftions on the fubject of the clandeftine trade,

·trade, in which a claufe was inferted, propofing to remove certain reftrictions in the act of 1781, which did not anfwer the defign of prevention, but became the occafion of immoral deviations and of difregard to the laws.

To referve to the Company the exclufive right of exporting marine ftores (which was among the fuggeftions), as mafts, fpars, cordage, anchors, pitch, tar, and alfo the right of exporting copper, was going a great way indeed to indulge them; for this gave them the exclufive fupply of that which they never had yet fupplied India with, and moft probably never would. Of two thoufand tons *per annum* of the article of marine ftores alone confumed by the country fhips in India, the Company, on inveftigation in 1791, had never fupplied two hundred tons: Indeed, fo far from it, that their own marine was in a great degree fupplied by clandeftine traders.

We then come to a Memoril which, on the 25th of March, the Chairman ufhered into the Committee of correfpondence from gentlemen, who, he faid, fubfcribed themfelves, " A Com-

F   mittee

mittee appointed by several mercantile houses, acting as agents for the East-Indies." The official letter which accompanies it from the committee, consisting of three of the most respectable houses in London, *viz.* Messrs. Muilman and Co. Boehm and Co. and Raikes and Co. does not appear, nor indeed, was it brought forward afterwards in the general court. Why this sort of mystery should be observed with an official letter, which ought to be as public as the day, is unaccountable. The first remark the committee make is, " that the Memoralists *avow themselves* to have set the laws of this country at defiance, and to have been agents in carrying on an illicit trade; although, in the seventh paragraph of their reasons in support of their Memorial, they very pathetically reprobate a disregard to the laws of this country, as a practice that has a degrading effect upon those who embark in it."

Now, very unfortunately for the Committee of Correspondence, this Memorial is afterwards printed by order of the Court of Directors, and *there is not one word in it tending to such an avowal.* In the answer of the Committee of Correspondence,

dence, they appear in like manner to mifappre-
hend the Memorialifts meaning almoft through-
out, nor do they feem, in any one part of it, to
invalidate a fingle argument advanced.

The Memorial in fact has much the fame tend-
ency as the other petitions, which appear from
different public bodies, for giving more facility
to the commerce between Britain and India, and
only differs in the following points:—As large
proprietors, the Memorialifts are attached to the
Company's real intereft, which intereft, from
the fubftance of the Memorial, they feem to have
ftudied with fuccefs: In confequence of this, it
appears to be their wifh that the Company fhould
remain in poffeffion of every exclufive privilege
which can be ufeful to them, and not detrimental
to the ftate.

Their principal aim avowedly is, and really
appears to be, " to annihilate completely the
clandeftine trade, and bring an equal trade in a
legal way into the Thames;" and they certainly

do

do point out the moſt effectual means for theſe ends.

An impartial reader of that Memorial, and of the Court's anſwer to it, who was a complete judge of the ſubject, would moſt probably view the Memorialiſts as the greateſt enemies the clandeſtine trade could have, and the Court of Directors the ſteady, though perhaps unintentional, ſupporters of it.

The Memorialiſts have the advantage of cool diſpaſſionate reaſoning alſo; whereas the Court, from their firſt ſetting off, ſeem to be very intemperate, as if they were attacked in their juſt rights by a ſet of ſmugglers.

As the writers have given a ſort of explanation of their Memorial, in conſequence of the Court's miſapprehenſion, we need ſay no more on the ſubject, as it will, no doubt, be publiſhed by the Court, and ſo ſpeak for itſelf.

There

There are certain principles in commerce which are so well known, and which repeatedly appear in these papers, that it would be superfluous to mention them here, were it not that the Court has entirely overlooked them, and has objected so strongly to giving the great mercantile interest of Britain the freedom required for it, which has appeared to be the only object that Administration could not give up.

One of these principles is, " That, provided the same quantity of India goods must be imported annually into Europe (and this the Company cannot prevent), the greater the quantity and the greater the variety which can be brought to any one port, the sales not only of these India goods at such port must be proportionally higher than at any other port, but the demand also of all other goods must likewise increase; for the increased number of purchasers, which such a variety of India goods must bring, cannot confine their purchases to any one sort of goods."

Another

Another position is, " That no mercantile body trading on their own capital, and paying intereſt and inſurance, can rival a ſimilar body trading upon a capital on which they neither have to pay intereſt nor inſurance, provided the management is equally good."

We would apply this fairly to the ſtate and circumſtances of the Company, without ſtraining it beyond its proper import. We admit that private traders may enhance the prices of India commodities at the original markets; but they cannot poſſeſs themſelves of the Company's aurung eſtabliſhmens, nor of a gratuitous capital. If they injure the Company, they muſt injure themſelves more; they cannot maintain a competition againſt them; the territorial revenues muſt weigh down all oppoſition, and the ſources of theſe are fed afreſh by every enhancement of the prices of thoſe commodities which the territories furniſh. We do not wiſh that any diſturbance ſhould be given to the Company's purchaſes abroad; means, we think, may be taken to obviate that conſequence; but it is

eaſy

eafy to fee that, in the affair of competition, the Company are not only incomparably the ftronger party for carrying it on, but the party that will gain *as fovereigns*, by their own lofs and the lofs of others *as merchants*. No alarming apprehen‐ fion, therefore, ought to be entertained from this quarter.

Having ftated the fubftance of what paffed in negotiation refpecting the clandeftine trade, and entered into fome difcuffion of the merits of that queftion, we are next led to the claim advanced by the Britifh manufacturers, " that the wear of Indian muflins and callicoes fhould be prohibited in this country;" and this fubject, though in our humble opinion important, lies in a fmall compafs. The Court of Directors, in their minute of the 25th of March, had actually conceded this point to the manufacturers: The minifter, however, apparently aware of its confequence to different interefts, was not fo ready to yield it, had ex‐ prefly left it open in his letter of the 26th of March; and the general Court of Proprietors which met on the 28th, alarmed at the afpect it

2   had

had on their affairs, refisted it with far more earneftnefs than they have fhewn in the queftion of the clandeftine trade. How does Mr. Dundas then ftand at prefent with refpect to it? In the very letter which conveyed the propofed prohibition, he fays, " I am aware that matter will, at the inftance of thofe immediately interefted, undergo a farther confideration; *and as I am perfectly perfuaded, on the moft mature confideration I can give to the fubject, that thofe who urge the requeft are acting in too narrow a view of it, I think it highly probable that part of the queftion may admit a revifion, with the acquiefcence of the gentlemen who have preffed it upon us.*" Is any thing more wanting to explain the ftate of this affair? Are many words neceffary to fhew that in fact there is no conteft here, that the Minifter is with the Court of Proprietors, and that, having already declared themfelves upon it, they will in the iffue receive due fatisfaction concerning it? Let us beware therefore of aggravating our differences into a mafs, by throwing among them things that in fact conftitute no part of them. Of

this

this defcription is the prefent fubject, and the
proprietors have reafon to congratulate themfelves, that it is not in reality a matter of feri-
ous contention.

There are three other points relative to trade in
difpute between the Court 'and Mr. Dundas.
Thefe are, firft, Whether the freight of privileged
goods fent by individuals on the Company's fhips,
agreed to be in all 20l. per ton, fhall be charged
in the proportion of 5l. on the *outward* ·bound
goods, and 15l. on the *homeward* bound, as he
thinks would be beft; or in the proportion of 8l.
outward, and 12l. homeward, as they require? Secondly, Whether the Company's charges on thofe
goods fhall be three *per cent.* as he propofes, or
five *per cent.* which the Chairman contended for?
And, laftly, Whether, among the merchandize fo
privileged by the Company with tonnage in their
fhips, *piece goods from India* fhall be included?

Now, it may be very well to pay a juft attention even to minute things; but fhall fuch

trivial

trivial points as these be the occasion of serious disagreement, and frustrate or obstruct a negotiation, which involves the fate of the first commercial body in the world, and most materially the welfare of this nation and of all Indostan? It is astonishing that any colour should be afforded for making this a question. In reality the Directors appear to be arguing against the interest of the Company, since the probability of a continued large importation from India to England is far greater than the probability of a continued large exportation *to* India. But what, if it should prove otherwise? and the Company should have 3l. per ton less than they require on outward bound goods, counterbalanced by 3l. more than they require on the homeward bound?—What if (contrary to probability) something should be lost by this arrangement, would it not be better to submit to the loss, than to put off the settlement of the charter and the parliamentary confirmation of our expected ten *per cent.* another year, and perhaps for ever? Is it for such points as these that we are to quarrel with an Administration

miniſtration which laid ſo liberal a baſis of negotiation ? As to the *charges* on privileged
goods, it need only be ſaid, that the Court, in
contending for 5 *per cent.* are confeſſedly contending for a profit; and the deſign of the mi-
niſter is, by holding forth all practicable induce-
ments to the Britiſh reſidents in India, to deſtroy
the clandeſtine trade, and bring their conſign-
ments to this country.

With reſpect to the third article, the excluſion
of piece goods from the merchandize which individuals ſhall be permitted to ſend home, it may
ſuffice to ſay, *that this is a new requiſition* on the
part of the Directors. For the ſeven laſt years,
this permiſſion has been conſtantly accorded when
the Company had any freight to ſpare; *and if the
great Indian ſtaple of piece goods is to be excluded
from the private imports into Britain; what is this,
in other words, but ſtill uphɔlding the clandeſtine trade?*
If that article is not allowed to come to England,
it will go, as it has too much done for a number
of years paſt, to all the ports of the continent;

and

and the other meafures now brought forward for aboliſhing illicit traffic will be fruſtrated. It muſt be once more repeated, that the confumption and demand of Europe for India commodities will not be leſſened by any reſtraints we lay on *our* importations, and it is moſt of all needful, when we propoſe to encourage an increaſed exportation from this country, that we ſhould enlarge the means of return in proportion. To increaſe our exports by means of individuals, and, at the fame time, narrow the former channel of private importation from India, what is it but an effectual contrivance to throw more than ever of the valuable trade in piece goods into foreign and irregular channels ? The Directors fay, that " if the piece good trade is opened, it will be impoſſible to gueſs how far ſpeculation may go, in extending it to very ruinous lengths," ſo as (according to their ſubſequent expreſſion) to " render it impoſſible for the Company to liquidate their political debts, ſtill leſs to furniſh the propoſed participation to the public." But *is not* the piece

good

good trade *now open?*—Has it not been open
thefe feven years? If any thing new were propofed, a fear of fpeculation might indeed be
pleaded; but this is an old bufinefs, a thing already practifed; and has it hurt the Company's
fales? Do they find a progreffive decreafe, or a
progreffive increafe, in the profits of their piece
goods for fome years paft? Befides, will private
fpeculations, that are unprofitable, long continue?
And if they prove advantageous, will not the
Company alfo gain? And what, after the utmoft
efforts that can be ufed, are the whole of the
profits on the Company's piece goods, that any
poffible variation in that article fhould materially
affect the refources of the Company, or the
participation founded upon it; which, after all,
is to fail firft, with refpect to the *fhare of govern-
weut only*, if it fails at all? We earneftly depre-
cate, therefore, *this new meafure of reftriction*, well
intended, we fhall readily admit, but very unhappily conceived for the interefts which all parties
wifh to promote.

One

One more point remains to be noticed, which turns rather upon the conftruction of what has already paffed, than upon an original difference in principle. It was underftood that, out of the 1,200,000l. calculated to be the annual furplus of the Company's affairs, an increafe in the dividend of two *per cent.*, making in all ten *per cent.*, fhould be allowed to the proprietors; 500,000l. more paid in liquidation of debt, and 500,000l. more, or any furplus that remained, not exceeding that fum, to Government.

The refolution propofed by Mr. Dundas touching this article, bears, that, if the profits of the Company in any one year fhall not fuffice for the payment of 500,000l. to Government, the deficiency fhall be made good from the furplus that may remain in any other year, after providing for the payment of dividend and of debt as above mentioned. The Court obferve hereupon, " that to make good this fum at all events, and create any deficiency as a debt, may be ruinous to the Company, and goes beyond any fair expectation

of

of the public, which ought not to exceed the Company's annual ability."

Now, the Adminiſtration and the Company both agree, that if, after the other ſpecified proviſions, the Company's ſurplus can afford 500,000l. annually to the public, the public ſhall have it. Then if the Company, after furniſhing the other allotted payments, have in one year a ſurplus of only 300,000l., and, in the next, a ſurplus of 700,000l., is it to be underſtood that, in theſe two years, Government ſhall receive only 800,000l. although, in faƈt, the Company have a ſurplus of 1,000,000l. ? Would this fairly and ſubſtantially fulfil the ſenſe of the firſt agreement between Adminiſtration and the Direƈtors ? And in what manner are we to underſtand that the claim of Adminiſtration *turns deficiency into a debt?* Is it a debt upon the general property of the Company, or a debt only upon a certain contingent ſurplus? The laſt merely, and the debt is no otherwiſe claimable than on the condition that the Company do aƈtually realiſe ſuch a ſurplus.

We

We fee, therefore, no poffibility of this claim's becoming "ruinous to the Company," fince it is founded folely upon a computation of profit; and the failure of this computation is a difcharge to the Company *.

After reviewing, then, every point of any importance, which has been the occafion of difputation between Adminiftration and the Court of Directors, we fee none refolvable into a fettled

---

* Indeed, when it is well confidered that any participation by Government is wholly fufpended on a contingent fund, whence alfo other large allotments are firft to be fatisfied, it muft be allowed that this gives the nation an additional claim to the entire fum ftipulated for it, if that fund can make it good.

.The liberality of Adminiftration alfo appears in the difpofal of the furplus remaining after the appropriations already mentioned, and after the Company's debts are reduced to 3,000,000l. in India, and the bond debt at home to 1,500,000l. viz. one fixth of the furplus they propofe to go in increafe to the dividend on the Company's ftock, and the other five-fixths, though to go to Government, *are yet to reft with them as a collateral fecurity for the Company's ftock and their dividends.*

difference

difference of opinion, except thofe which relate
to the private and clandeftine trades; and even
with refpect to thefe, only the articles which are
trifling, fuch as the allotment of the agreed rate of
freight, and the difference of two *per cent.* in the ·
charges, remain matters of conteft; for, with
regard to the more important queftions of bringing the trade, now clandeftine, to the port of
London, all parties declare for it: And, with regard to the only other queftion remaining upon
this fubject, whether Britifh refidents in India
fhall be permitted to receive commiffions from
foreigners, the Committee of Correfpondence have
given an opinion upon it, which, in our humble
conception, may ferve as the bafis of regulation
refpecting this matter: " The Committee are
perfuaded, under the circumftances they have
ftated, that any permiffion to be extended to foreigners, or their trade, will be confined to India:
That no perfon fhall be permitted to act as an
agent to foreigners, or others, who is not under
covenants to the Company, and under the entire
control and authority of the governments in

H   India:

India: That no Britifh agent fhall be fuffered to lend, on advance, money for the benefit of foreigners in trade; nor to trade themfelves to any place whatfoever on this fide the Cape of Good Hope, except to Great Britain: And, finally, that fuch agents fhall not be permitted to interfere at the Aurungs in the purchafe of piecegoods."

It appears extremely proper that the Company's power of licenfing and controlling all Britifh fubjects in their territorial poffeffions fhould be continued; and that all exifting acts and regulations, *legiflative or local*, touching the refidence of fuch fubjects, and the mode of conducting manufacturing and aurung bufinefs in the country, fhould remain in force.

Here likewife, therefore, there is, in fact, nothing effential to adjuft; and it appears aftonifhing that a matter of fuch little real importance as the propofed alteration in the act of 21 George III. refpecting intercourfe with foreigners, fhould have

become

become the oftenfible caufe of alienation between his Majefty's Minifters and the reprefentatives of the Company. That act had its origin on the laft renewal of the charter in 1781. It was apparently intended to prevent the affiftance of Britifh fub-jects from extending, in any poffible way, to the trade of European foreigners in India or Europe. It is univerfally notorious that the act has not anfwered its end. Some, indeed, have refpected the authority, though they faw the impolicy, of of the law. The fervants of the Company, more efpecially thofe diftinguifhed by their character or truft, have moreover been actuated by a fenfe of honour in refpect to themfelves and to their employ-ers. But they were the very perfons in whom a power of dealing with foreigners could moft fafely have been vefted, becaufe fuperior ties of intereft, reputation, and attachment, would ftill have main-tained in their minds a due regard to thofe inte-refts of the Company, to prevent the apprehended facrifice of which, the reftrictions in queftion were framed. Others, either not under the fame cove-nants, or not entirely under the fame influences, have always been found to act as the agents of fo-

reigners,

reigners, and the clandestine trade has greatly increased since the act was passed. Foreigners find no difficulties; the act is daily trampled upon, and the consciousness of transgressing, in one instance, the example exhibited to the world, of transgressing with impunity, tends to diffuse a spirit of irregularity and licence unfavourable to morals and to society.——Now what can be more natural and proper than to advert to this state of things upon the formation of a new charter? Would it have been right to have passed over without regard an inveterate disorder, growing with time still more inveterate? If the law is good, and if it can be rendered effective, let it by all means be enforced. The policy of the law has been strongly denied by persons who ought to be competent judges; but all agree that, after an experience of twelve years, it proves ineffective, nor does any one expect that it will hereafter be better enforced than it has been. Shall it then be continued merely to be slighted, when all hope of its answering its professed design is gone, and when it only serves to injure men's minds? No answer to this capital objection
tion

tion has been attempted on the part of the Court of Directors. But if this objection be indeed founded, what are they contending for in their violent refiftance to the repeal of this law? Are they combating againft a *new evil*, which only the abrogation of this law will introduce; or are they ftickling about the dead letter of a ftatute, confcious that the reality of the evil already exifts, and that this ftatute is efficacious to no end but thofe detrimental confequences already ftated? If this be fo, ought it not to be done away, and other means ufed to accomplifh its defign? Thefe means are indeed already agreed upon in the fcheme of bringing the trade, now clandeftine, to the port of London: Surely, therefore, the point here in queftion is not a caufe for which the Company would chufe to hazard, or to poftpone the renewal of their charter, with all the benefits fufpended upon it. And as in fact there appears to be no folid obftacle to the profecution of the negotiation, let us hope that it will go on without further delay, and foon be happily terminated.

APPEN-

APPENDIX.

Exports *from* Europe *to* India.

THE Exports of Europe to India are annually about 37,454 tons, and may be claffed under the following heads :

First : *Foreign Companies,* viz.

Dutch, French, Danifh, Portuguefe, regular
 fhips, -   -   -   -   18,048 tons

Second : *Clandeftine Trade.*

Englifh commerce carried on under foreign
 flags, -   -   -   -   10,255

Third : *Private Trade.*

In Englifh Company's fhips, carried by commanders and officers licenfed and unlicenfed, on an average of ten years to 1790, -   -   -   -   4,258

Fourth : *Englifh Company's.*

On an average of the laft fix years, ending in 1790; during which period their exports have been increafed beyond that of any former period :

      Goods for fale,   2748
      Stores, -   - 2145
                ——   4,893

    Annual European Exports to India,   37,454 tons.

THE END.